MERGERS & ACQUISITIONS PLAYBOOK

A technical book with Case Studies

RICHARD A. BOYSEN

outskirts
press

Mergers & Acquisitions Playbook
A technical book with Case Studies
All Rights Reserved.
Copyright © 2022 Richard A Boysen
v1.0

The opinions expressed in this manuscript are solely the opinions of the author and do not represent the opinions or thoughts of the publisher. The author has represented and warranted full ownership and/or legal right to publish all the materials in this book.

This book may not be reproduced, transmitted, or stored in whole or in part by any means, including graphic, electronic, or mechanical without the express written consent of the publisher except in the case of brief quotations embodied in critical articles and reviews.

Outskirts Press, Inc.
http://www.outskirtspress.com

ISBN: 978-1-9772-5187-9

Cover Photo © 2022 www.gettyimages.com. All rights reserved - used with permission.

Outskirts Press and the "OP" logo are trademarks belonging to Outskirts Press, Inc.

PRINTED IN THE UNITED STATES OF AMERICA

Author Caveat

The purchase of this book does not constitute a consulting or advisory agreement between the buyer or reader and the author and or RAB Financial Advisors, LLC

Table of Contents

Foreword — i

Chapter 1 Fundamentals — 1

Chapter 2 Things to Consider Before Due Diligence — 7

Chapter 3 Mentoring — 10

Chapter 4 Acquisitions by Purchase, Merger, Joint Venture or Leveraged Buyout — 13

Chapter 5 Raising Capital — 29

Chapter 6 Sales Process — 31

Chapter 7 Working with Japanese Clients — 46

Chapter 8 Beef Company Transaction — 50

Chapter 9 Perils of Falling in Love with an Opportunity — 55

Chapter 10 Community Newspapers — 58

Chapter 11 Working with Entrepreneurs — 61

Chapter 12 Working with Strategic Buyers — 67

Conclusion — 73

Acknowledgements — 74

Foreword

I am passing through the twilight of my career as a Merger & Acquisitions (M&A) strategy consultant.

It began in 1968 as a part-time intern with the Dallas office of what then was Haskins & Sells. After spending my internship working in auditing and taxes and completing my bachelor's degree in accounting at Southern Methodist University, I decided taxation was more suitable for me since the independence rules of public accountancy, as then applied to tax practice, allowed more leeway for client advocacy.

Hindsight proved this was the ideal choice for me since I was part of the tax team that structured the merger of two of the largest companies in North Central Texas. This transaction caused more tax law changes than any previous merger in the United States: I had a newly-found appreciation for the ways in which tax knowledge could add value for clients and enhance career prospects.

My mother encouraged me to find a career where I could do what I loved best. I found it in M&A strategy consulting.

I am writing this as a "how to" book which includes several case studies. I use a conversational approach where I share what I learned during my career. What I enjoyed most was meeting and working with intelligent people having diverse experiential backgrounds. If you are a good listener, much can be learned at no charge.

I do not disclose names of the parties or companies involved unless the deals were public, I obtained consent, or the parties are no longer living. I made this decision since ethics are an important part of all life and non-disclosure is assumed for all business transactions.

Most of my transactions were in the $30 to $200 million range. While I include, as a case study, work with one "startup" venture, I am not including startups as part of the "how to" part of my book.

CHAPTER 1

Fundamentals

Mergers & Acquisitions consulting is *always* about adding, preserving, or protecting value. Merger and Acquisition (M&A) deals are hard work: nerve-wracking, financially and emotionally costly, disruptive to the businesses involved, and often fail to produce hoped-for results. According to a recent study published by Investopedia measuring completed deals in excess of $100 million, the post transaction price increase was about 1.7 percent higher than stock market indices. If you or your client lack a high degree of confidence in the outcome, it is best to think about something else.

Useful sources for learning more about the fundamentals mentioned include: *Joint Ventures Theoretical and Empirical Perspectives B. Kogut -Strategic Management Journal, 1988 Wiley Online Library, Perceptions of organizational change: A stress and coping perspective AE Rafferty, MA Griffin Journal of applied psychology, 2006.*

A useful conversation starter I used when meeting a Board Chair, CEO, COO, or CFO considering a transaction was asking about business factors that kept them up at night. If you ask this type of question when it is not anticipated, you receive first impressions.

Since these are unfiltered by previous thought or analysis, they constitute a helpful starting point. Too often you find they have only focused on the upside. When this happens your role, by professional necessity, becomes, to some extent, that of a devil's advocate.

Transaction expectation failures result from a variety of causes.

People issues are at the top of my list; One analogy is the military situation where generals set the strategy and the chiefs, who represent the boots on the ground, select the tactics. Human nature kicks in and individual and group priorities such as what happens to me and my people take control of the process. Similarly, in the live theater business, the role of the director is to set and refine the process and check in frequently during the run of the play to make sure the cast is not going off script. A similar role should be taken by a key person on the transaction team.

A second reason involves unrealistic synergy assumptions: two plus two is far too often expected to equal fifteen. Factors impacting the harvesting of synergies include people issues, competitor reactions, and regulatory issues. An important factor for cross border transactions includes the government will for the industry, e.g., how might the local government in, for example, China react to a technology business? Other significant issues involving cross border deals include currency volatility and its impact on future financial statement and rules regarding employee benefits.

A third reason includes situations where the acquirer chooses to clone the acquired company in its image.

In 1978 A Publicly owned Telecom company (PT)acquired a company that manufactured long-distance switches for phone company networks and was believed to be a great fit with PT. Immediately after closing the purchase, PT began changing the acquired company's culture; many of the acquired company's people jumped ship. As part of the deal, the acquired company's former board chair was added to PT's board receiving an annual $40,000 board membership fee. At some point PT's management decided to save money by ending the relationship. In less than 60 days, the former board chair secured the financing to buy a switch manufacturing company that hired most of the acquired company' management, and a new competitor was born. PT, by saving $40,000 pretax, created a competitor that quickly destroyed the value of its investment in the acquired company.

This is a great example of corporate hubris destroying value

Given the lack of certainty that a transaction will fulfill expectations, you might reasonably ask why the company and its people should be subjected to the intellectual, emotional and financial stress involved.

My experience shows that a complex array of substantive and intangible concepts are in play.

Necessity is involved where owners believe they must make a deal to maintain competitive advantage or block a new technology.

For example, around 2012 several auto manufacturers announced that they would use carbon fiber flywheels in some of their 2014 models. Carbon fiber's relative strength made it possible to build a battery offering gas mileage equal to or exceeding that achieved by hybrids such as the Toyota Prius and Highlander.

A carbon fiber flywheel is essentially a mechanical battery that stores kinetic energy in a rotating mass. Advanced power electronics and a motor/generator convert that kinetic energy to electric energy, making it instantly available when needed. These systems are modular and can be configured to meet the power capacity demands of a variety of applications, from 100 kW to multi-MW systems.

The principal benefit of this device is offering gas mileage equivalent to a hybrid without the environmental impact of traction batteries.

Has anyone seen a car offering a carbon fiber flywheel? Who might have purchased this technology so they could continue selling gasoline or diesel undiminished by the impact of carbon fiber flywheels?

Other deals happen so that buyers can increase revenue and market share. The acquisition of a Satellite television company by a large telecom company fits in this category. Similarly, one should look for more consolidation as streaming video begins taking revenue from cable and satellite providers. In people centric industries and professions, one might expect consolidation transactions involving firms active in finance, legal, software, video gaming, consulting and hardware development.

A 2008 Price Waterhouse Coopers survey showed the following transaction reasons and the percentage of transactions where each was a key factor:

New market access	76%
Growth in market share	74%
New products	54%
Access to talent	47%
Enhanced reputation	46%
Reducing operating costs	46%
Distribution Channels	38%
Access to new technologies	26%

| Reduction in competitors | 26% |
| Access to new brands | 25% |

There are other reasons for seeking acquisitions, but I close this topic with the macho rationale.

Bigger is often better. If the metrics of revenue, net income, and or assets of the company increase, better compensation must surely follow. This is reasonable expectation since many compensation committees use them for setting senior management salaries, stock options, and bonuses. This is how capitalism works. Size matters in many industries.

For example, ignoring personality issues, how might Tesla have fared had it gained access to the capital of a major automobile company? Of course, many question how big is too big. Did General Electric become too sprawling for management effectiveness or did its problems relate to the departure of a very talented top manager?

Finally, with a successful transaction many people get to experience the extreme joy and pride from making something better than they found it.

Optimum value creation, enhancement and protection occurs when your team has the most competent people.

Due diligence, transaction structuring, and post-acquisition integration are basic tasks for maximizing the value of any deal.

Due diligence is auditing on steroids. It is auditing plus projecting future results based on discussions with customers, lenders, suppliers, key management, and reviewing the industry outlook. Other tasks include reviewing customer and vendor financial stability, personnel files and the company's credit history and capacity. Adequate due diligence is far more than reading the auditor's report.

Years ago, I attended a board meeting of a European company that is among the largest huge scale (bridges and stadiums) contractors in the world. I was there to present initial findings on a North American firm they wished to acquire. I concluded my presentation by recommending they perform due diligence. The board chair said this was unnecessary as they had copies of the auditor's report. I told him the reports were only good at the time of the report and did not include current status and estimated future financial performance. They did not pay for or perform any kind of due diligence; they were disappointed when the transaction did not produce the hoped-for operating results.

The advisor and the client should assemble the best team possible. The team should include people having the following skills: due diligence, accounting structuring, tax structuring, relevant industry experience, valuation, employee benefit plans, and negotiating. In specialized industries such as insurance and banking, using actuaries and professionals having loan reserve expertise is essential.

CHAPTER 2

Things to Consider Before Due Diligence

Not falling in love with the deal. Far too often acquirers view a deal as being the remedy for all of the company's woes. Combining weak companies solves nothing and has the potential for creating newer and more significant operating, financial, and human resource issues.

Consider the merger of the two largest Banks in Texas. Hoping for better results from the combination, the firms merged in the late 1980s and failed within one year. A team visited the Bank's CFO and COO which told them its analysis indicated that the Bank would run out of cash within 30 days. They asked the team to leave; less than 3 weeks later, the Bank was taken down by the FDIC.

Banking has its specific set of challenges including lending, investing, regulations, growth strategy and people. The same is true for manufacturers and producers. Regardless of the industry, it seldom makes sense to combine under-performing companies.

Another example pertinent to not falling in love is the case where my firm's M&A Strategy Consulting group was retained by a large buyout group to help with due diligence for a regional chain of movie theaters. Our client told me all of the large financial buyers were bidding. They were all in love with the deal. My experience on this opportunity showed that while MBAs could do the numbers, some often failed to properly interpret them. The successful financial buyer ended up putting the property into bankruptcy within three years of purchase. Love is often destructive.

The next step is finding the best talent available. Often, this requires including people with other firms having essential industry experience.

Financial and tax due diligence are always important. While in the firm's Dallas office, I had the opportunity to work with Clem S who was the best audit partner I worked with during my 30 plus year career. When I transferred to the firm's Los Angeles office, I called him, telling him the industry involved in the transaction and asking whether he had time to look at the deal and identify possible deal traps. There was never a time when he did not find issues that other people on the team missed. He was a consummate professional; I miss having access to his wisdom.

While my professional background is in taxation, I always used other tax professionals for tax due diligence. A favorite was Ed L a tax principal in the Los Angeles office. Ed passed a few years ago; his keen insights are missed.

Operations due diligence is a key M&A skill. I was fortunate to learn the basics of operations due diligence during my time at Akzona Inc. in Asheville, NC. Akzona owned businesses producing yarn, salt mining, pharmaceuticals, animal hide processing, and cable and wire manufacturing. Having this background helped me lead deals in fields outside my primary skill of tax structuring.

Many years ago Haskins and Sells published an annual summary of accounting and tax articles. Their premise was that accounting is an art as well as a science. Knowing when to walk away from a prospective deal is an art. The science part includes the numbers and what they mean. The art is interpreting. There are many deals people wish they had made and many that were completed to their regret. Is it all luck? In some cases it is. To supplement or mitigate the "luck factor" you must know deep inside yourself that nothing of value is ever achieved without hard work and to be cheerful in all weather. One never dies from a deal that goes south, though one might wish they had. Good luck!

CHAPTER 3

Mentoring

As part of a later chapter I mention the importance of fielding the best team available.

Mentoring and being mentored are important parts of career development and creating the best team. People who are good coaches and teachers have the basic skills for mentoring. Excellent mentors help people perform at their best.

I was fortunate to have three mentors during my professional career.

The first was Leon M, a tax principal in the firm where I began my career.

When I got my first job that was not delivering newspapers or being a Russian Linguist in the United States Air Force Security Service, my father told me to go to work, keep the required hours, keep my head down, and go home.

After about 60 days with the firm, Leon invited me to lunch. He opened the conversation by telling me I was one of a very few new hires that did not go to him seeking answers. What I did was find several alternatives and request his opinion regarding the best one. He told me I clearly had the talent to become a partner; if I did not it would be my fault. When I asked why, he said if people do not know you, they will not trust you. He proceeded to tell me that if I failed to improve my communication skills, he would not give me any clients. I quickly became the male version of "Chatty Kathy" which was key to my ultimately becoming a partner.

The Second mentor was Frank G, Tax Partner with my second CPA firm. From him I learned that it was good to get to know my co-workers; whether they were married and whether they had children. I also learned to shake hands with everyone I met including administrators, maids and porters.

My third mentor was Marvin S, founder of a steel company, in rural, Texas. My key learning from him was knowing to only promote people to supervisory positions who knew how to properly treat people: you can demand much, but you must treat their person with respect. If you cannot, you must ask them to move on. I also experienced the joy of working with an entrepreneur.

I suggested that his company adopt the last in first out method (LIFO) for valuing manufacturing plant inventories. The method I chose was component cost which has the best opportunity to maximize tax deferral and after-tax cash flow. While working there, I used my enhanced communication skills to become friendly with Marvin. Whenever I was visiting, he invited me to dinner at his home.

One evening I asked him how someone from Brooklyn founded a Rebar Fabrication Plant in rural Texas. He told me he returned from fighting Germans for six years during World War II and was going to enroll at City College of New York. On his way into the building, he met a friend who recently returned from military service. He asked the friend if he had enrolled. The friend said he had not, but had merely picked up his transcript and was going to Texas. When asking why, the friend replied that Texas was a whole lot different from Brooklyn. They drove to Texas that next morning. Finding jobs, they saved up money and with $500, Marvin bought a cornfield where he built a steel mill using melted scrap metal to form rebar used for road construction.

This was the first time I experienced to joy of working with an entrepreneur.

I enjoyed and profited from having outstanding mentors. During my career, I repaid them by mentoring many people who worked as part of my group. Over time I began to include potential mentoring skills as part of my hiring criteria.

CHAPTER 4

Acquisitions by Purchase, Merger, Joint Venture or Leveraged Buyout

Basic Terms

A **merger** is a combination of two or more companies into a new company (NEWCO)

A **Purchase** is either a purchase of a legal entity or its assets. If it is a purchase of the entity, that entity becomes a subsidiary of the purchaser. Asset purchases result in either a new division of the purchaser or new assets of an existing business. If a new division, it has separate financial statements.

A **Joint Venture (JV)** results in a new legal entity, generally a partnership or Limited Liability Company established by capital (cash and or real, tangible, and intangible property) contributed by the JV participants.

Legal, tax and financial accounting issues often determine the form selected for the transaction. You should note that, unless publicly traded, joint ventures are controlled by contract agreements and not under securities laws.

A **Leveraged Buyout** is a purchase where a large portion of the purchase price is composed of long-term debt secured by the fixed assets and anticipated cash flows.

Ethics - practitioners should avoid even the appearance of insider trading. I never invested in anything other than exchange traded or mutual funds while I lead my M&A group.

Confidentiality - of Client information is fundamental to M&A practice. I had to fire an individual for disclosing client information to a prospective buyer without the client's permission.

The Acquisition Process

At some point, management might wish to retain outside assistance. The benefits would include keeping management's internal resources focused on daily tasks and having a third party's opinion on various options selected. An outside resource could prevent costly mistakes such as the following.

Years ago, a poultry producer wished to get into downstream poultry processing and, without informing a publicly traded processing company, purchased ten percent of its outstanding stock. What made things worse was that the stock acquisition funds were made as a demand loan from the public company's primary lender. The lender demanded payment; the company declared bankruptcy in the hope that it would provide time to work things out with the public company.

An outside advisor would have suggested meeting with the public company to discuss ways they might work together to achieve mutual goals. This would have avoided the bankruptcy filing.

There are many instances where companies have done very well without outside advisors. I will mention one, as a case study, in my chapter on the acquisition of a meat packing plant in the Pacific Northwest.

Strategy Development

Strategy development includes analyzing the company's strengths, weaknesses, opportunities, and threats (SWOT).

Senior operating and financial leaders should comprise SWOT team membership. If the company has a board chair who is not the CEO it makes sense that the chair not be involved since that person is responsible for oversight. If the roles are combined, that person should not be on the team.

If the strategic goal is a new product line the tactics evaluated include build, buy, or joint venture. When the goal is talent acquisition, the tactics include direct hire (being aware of non-compete issues) and buying the company or its assets. The assets versus shares issue generally is determined with reference to tax and intellectual property matters.

The SWOT output includes a core competency analysis, a strategic direction, and a sense of the transaction size and complexity the organization can manage financially and with internal staffing.

This step also includes a preliminary implementation strategy, development of a fact base containing possible acquisition targets, determining means of obtaining introductions and, where applicable, the best approach to building from within.

Target Screening

Listed companies are easiest as Forms 10-K are readily available as are analyst reports. Financial publications, including *Barrons, Wall Street Journal, Wall Street Transcript*, and *The Economist Magazine* have helpful company and industry specific reports providing useful background information.

Industry and company specific data for private companies can be found using a data base service such as *Fact Set*; a paid subscription service offering a wealth of data useful for comparing the performance of targets with industry peers. Trade magazines are also helpful as are government industry reports accessible using North American Industry Classification System (NAICS) code. Industry specific Audit Guides used by the Internal Revenue service contain background useful for developing due diligence tasks.

The benefits from proactive target screening include; minimizing adverse selection, staying on script, i.e., not straying from strategic objectives, avoiding the risk of being involved in an auction, and learning how to work through the process and bring it to the best possible conclusion.

Preliminary Due Diligence

Completing this step provides more detailed insight regarding the target and how it might integrate into the company. Tasks include locating and interpreting available financial data and reviewing the target's key personnel using LinkedIn and similar social media resources. These are useful for reviewing skills and work histories. One red flag is key managers who jump from company to company.

Preliminary due diligence should continue until you are satisfied that the target is worth pursuing and bearing the financial and organization cost of final due diligence.

Projected Synergies and Value Drivers

While business combinations (mergers, acquisitions, joint ventures) seem driven by synergy hopes, most are used for increasing efficiency; which is a great reason. The art of dealing with synergies is determining the cost of capturing the value while not paying the seller for the value created by the combination.

- Principal value drivers include:
- Capital access
- Customer Base
- Scalability and economies of scale
- Profitability
- Marketing and brand strength
- People
- Technology
- Market Environment
- Product and service portfolio

The company's size and financial history provides a measure of its access to capital. A combination with a target having great capital access adds value and efficiency.

If the potential target's customer base overlaps with the company's, marketing and distribution synergies and efficiencies are possible.

Positive economies of scale and scalability provide opportunity for growth. What might result if one allocates increased capital resources to the target's business?

The target's marketing strategies and brand strength might add value to those of the acquirer, increasing combined enterprise value.

Overlaps in service and product offerings, human resources, and technology provide significant efficiencies for inclusion in the value estimates for the combined enterprise.

A detailed analysis of a potential target's value drivers provides a sense of the synergies and efficiencies possible through acquisition. They are useful for calculation post acquisition value but generally not included in the offer price analysis.

Negotiate Letter of Intent

The Letter of Intent (LOI) is a legal document produced by the business and legal members of the deal team. Although these documents are generally non-binding (as they are intended to just outline the intention to work in good faith to assess the viability of doing a deal) they are an important part of the process and the specificity of preparation is a form of art with key factors including the relative strengths of the parties and anticipated transaction complexity.

If the buyer really needs to make the deal, the LOI is often brief and less demanding. If the deal is complex due to the nature of the business and anticipated complexity of integrating the target into the newly combined business, greater specificity is used in that part of the LOI.

Buyers send a letter of intent (LOI) once their deal team agrees on a suitable acquisition target and offer price. Disclosure of any third-party funds required is part of the letter.

The LOI includes buyer's offer, price, proposed transaction process and timing: setting dates for completion of each part of the process and the extent of buyer due diligence. In smaller deals, the seller sets up a due diligence room having documents requested by buyer. Larger transactions use specialized third-party online facilities for due diligence.

If the transaction includes financing, a lender letter showing support of a bid at the offer price usually resolves seller concern about buyer's ability to complete the transaction.

In most deals in which I participated, legal counsel's past experience determined its choice of language used for bargaining and deal specificity.

Definitive Due Diligence

A great starting point for definitive due diligence is the target or its broker prepared pitch book. These documents present the company's financial position and prospects in the best light possible.

If prepared by an honest broker (there are more than a few) the only sins will be those of omission. Nevertheless, assume then verify.

Definitive Due Diligence begins when both parties agree on the negotiated version of the LOI. One determines its scope by reference to the transaction size and complexity.

As is the case when operating a transportation vehicle, the goal of definitive due diligence

is minimizing the possibility of injury and loss. In business transactions this is achievable when everything possibly knowable about the target business is known prior to signing a final contract.

The following illustrates the possible damage when what should have been known was not.

During the late 1980s two entrepreneurs began acquiring community newspapers. On one transaction they concluded the operations and financial due diligence for a Houston area group of papers and had their lenders meet with them and the sellers to obtain final loan consent and move on to closing the deal. Out of nowhere one of the lending group looked at a wall picture, asking "why do you have a picture of a gasoline station on your wall".

The response was that the property was a gasoline station thirty years previously. Everything came to a halt pending satisfactory completion of an environmental study. This was a serious diligence error of omission for which there were reasons but not credible excuses. To the relief of all parties, the study results were satisfactory, and closing was only delayed by two weeks.

Due diligence includes reviews of financial statements for at least the past five accounting years. Important documents include: all material contracts including leases, loans, supply agreements, purchase agreements, and contracts with governmental agencies, all tax reports including federal, state, local, foreign, payroll, and property taxes require close analysis.

The review of targets subject to regulation should include regulator reports and, when believed necessary, discussions with appropriate regulatory officials.

Employee benefit plan specialists and, where applicable, actuaries should review employment agreements, non-compete arrangements, and benefit plans to calculate the funding status and potential undisclosed liabilities.

If the target has offshore operations, discussions with the host government officials should reveal their will for the target's industry in their country.

The due diligence team generally includes lawyers and industry experts. Often companies will add appropriate third-party industry experts to their team. As due diligence progresses, buyers often find that the scope requires expansion and the use of additional outside resources.

ACQUISITIONS BY PURCHASE, MERGER, JOINT VENTURE OR LEVERAGED BUYOUT

Where the target has material purchase, supply, or employment agreements, interviews with the counterparties are essential.

Environmental experts should provide consultation for all target businesses not having recent environmental studies.

The fundamental purposes of reviewing target historical financial statements and tax returns include identifying or ascertaining:

- potential deferred maintenance
- hidden costs such as underfunded plans
- improper or inconsistent application of accounting principles and lax internal controls
- risks associated with related party transactions
- tax risks and tax opportunities

With privately-owned companies the owner's compensation structure, including amounts paid to or on behalf of family members is closely analyzed. Is the owner taking an amount sufficient to compensate a successor Chief Operating Officer (COO)? If not, the projections should show the need for increased salaries and bonuses. Is the owner taking more benefits than appropriate for a successor COO? In that event the projections would include a reduction in costs.

In many deals integration planning begins too late. It should start no later than the commencement of definitive due diligence. Integration is often the most complicated part of a deal; it is best to know how difficult it might be before finalizing a transaction.

Negotiating Final Transaction Structure

Tax and accounting issues generally drive selection of the chosen transaction structure.

Prior to June 30, 2000 buyers often tried to qualify for pooling of interests accounting so they would not have to amortize goodwill associated with the increase in value of the target company's assets.

However, with the elimination of this method of accounting for purchases, the accounting rules for goodwill changed from amortization to an annual test of its impairment. If no impairment, no write down on the financial statements which eliminated the need for pooling of interest structures.

Should one buy the company or its assets? If the company, the tax and accounting cost basis carries over. While it is possible to adjust the tax basis (IRC Section 334(b)(2) making appropriate elections, regulations limit flexibility. In asset purchases, once both parties agree to the asset values, those values generally control tax basis going forward.

In some situations, asset purchases are preferred by buyers since undisclosed liabilities remain with the seller.

Other reasons for asset purchases include:

Seller wishes to retain unrelated assets

Buyer prefers avoiding assumption of benefit plan and debt obligations

Uncertain environmental risks

Tax risks - Tax and accounting experts construct models showing the effects of the available alternatives on projected after-tax earnings

ACQUISITIONS BY PURCHASE, MERGER, JOINT VENTURE OR LEVERAGED BUYOUT

and financial statements.

Method of payment is part of the negotiations. Cash is always good; sometimes buyers and sellers wish to use debt (straight or convertible) preferred stock (straight or convertible) and different forms of contingent payments. A contingent payment makes sense when uncertainty exists with respect to estimated income and or cash flow. A common provision would provide additional payments if the target business beats projections by specified amounts.

Many deals fail to achieve anticipated results because buyers devote far too little time and effort to integration planning. Integration complexity varies with the transaction type.

Subsidiary bolt-on - This occurs when a subsidiary acquires a company in a related business. Difficulty is generally minimal since the subsidiary manages all integration without assistance from the parent company.

Function Integration – This includes integration of Accounting, Finance and Human Resources. Use of a specified time frame (e.g., 100 days) applies to this effort. Generally, buyers apply moderate effort to accomplish this integration.

Functional and Operational Integration – This often involves synergy and initiative planning and execution. Senior management applies time frames for completion. In this type of integration, complexity varies from moderate to substantial.

Full Integration – All functions integrated with substantial complexity. Dedicated functional support necessary, including synergy planning and execution.

I find the **Mergers & Acquisitions Integration Handbook** by Scott Whitaker, published by John Wiley & Sons in 2012 quite useful for integration planning and recommend it for use in all transactions.

Too often insufficient attention is paid to getting the best capital structure. Getting the capital structure right does not guarantee success, but a poor structure often causes failure with good deals.

Once definitive due diligence, transaction structure and integration plans are completed the parties negotiate a final purchase price. Findings in both steps affect value for both parties. As mentioned previously, this is where "art" comes into play. Should one walk away?

It is an old observation that leaders from both sides learn much about each other; how they feel about the deal and where leverage stands. If both sides agree on a final price, they execute a contract and move on to closing.

After closing the difficult task of integration begins.

I was a partner in the Dallas office a national CPA firm when it merged with a smaller national firm. Since ours was the larger firm, we received cash distributions in order that smaller firm's tax year end applied after the merger; resulting in a tax deferral for the new firm.

The four years following the merger were difficult. New people, new accounting systems and new approaches to doing business were stressful. I had to learn and live with new rules.

My takeaway from this experience is that people centric businesses are extremely difficult to integrate.

Ventures

A Joint Venture (JV) agreement is a product of intense legal negotiation.

The formation process is similar to that used in M&A transactions. Significant differences include:

JV relationships are based on contract as opposed to securities law

Due diligence needs include determining the effect of the potential relationship on each company's brand and business reputation

While the parties due not assume each other's financial liabilities, it seldom makes financial sense to partner with an entity having too much near or long-term debt.

Joint ventures are most frequently used in the petroleum industry. The largest example is **Arabian American Oil Company (Aramco)**, founded by the Standard Oil Co. of California (Chevron) in 1933, when the government of Saudi Arabia granted it a concession.

The use of JVs makes sense for this industry as it facilitates resource sharing among industry participants. Resources shared include capital, technology, geographic locations, and skilled personnel.

Geographic resources are financially and strategically important when used to avoid transporting petroleum products across countries or continents. An example includes situations where the JV members own storage and pipeline facilities in many countries. If a JV member located in the United States has a customer in Italy and a fellow member has a facility in Italy, the required product can be shipped from the Italian storage facility, eliminating the cost of shipping from the United States to Italy.

Other industries using joint ventures include technology, marketing and distribution, auto production (Toyota and Subaru on the BRZ model), and aircraft development and manufacturing (Airbus).

While almost any legal structure can be used for Joint Ventures, the form most often used is a partnership or limited liability company (LLC). LLCs are often used to limit the liability of the JV members. The use of partnerships or LLCs means that the taxable income generated by the JV passes through to its members who include the income, gains, losses and tax credits in their tax returns.

Another form of JV is the **Cooperative.** Businesses using the cooperative form include oil and gas and retail distribution.

The cooperative best known by the general public in the United States is Recreational Equipment, Inc. (REI). REI meets its applicable tax requirements by paying annual dividends based on each customer's purchases.

Cooperatives are subject to separate sets of federal and state income tax rules. In some business situations, these requirements make the cooperative venture form unattractive.

Leveraged Buyouts

A Leveraged Buyout (LBO) is commonly defined as a financial transaction in which a combination of equity and debt is used to purchase a company and the company's cash flow is used to service the new debt.

Successful examples include Safeway, Hilton Hotels, and Gibson Greeting Cards. Failures include the Southland Corporation and a myriad of privately-owned companies.

LBOs use the targeted company's assets and projected cash flows to obtain debt financing required to purchase the company. They are called hostile takeovers when management of the targeted company does not want the deal to go through. More LBOs occur when interest rates are low, reducing the cost of borrowing, and when a particular industry or company is underperforming and considered undervalued.

According to an article by Justin Walton published in *Investopedia* and updated in 2019, the ten largest LBOs were:

- Energy Future Holdings
- Hilton Hotels
- Clear Channel
- Kinder Morgan
- RJR Nabisco
- Freescale Semiconductor
- PetSmart
- Georgia Pacific
- Harrah's Entertainment
- First Data

Mr. Walton's article is a must read for anyone thinking about an LBO as it contains a brief summary of what happened in each of these transactions.

As is always the case in finance, art and science are keys to successful LBOs.

The art is divining (perhaps using a crystal ball) the future for the target industry and company. The science includes selecting the ratio of debt and equity that assures solvency while maximizing return on invested capital.

LBO transactions created fortunes for some and bankruptcy for others. In some cases, they destroyed hundreds and perhaps thousands of jobs and eviscerated employee benefit plans. They are, perhaps, the starkest representation of the good and evil of our capitalist system.

Carefully managing the due diligence process for LBOs minimizes costs until such time as the deal suitability is achieved. Often sponsors spend so much on due diligence that they feel unable to walk away from a potentially bad deal due to costs they are unwilling to write off.

CHAPTER 5

Raising Capital

Many M&A projects include finding capital (debt and or equity) for clients.

In some situations, sellers retain a percentage of the equity and or provide seller financing. This is generally good for both parties as it eliminates the need for broker fees and expenses as well as the cost of assembling pitch books for proposed investors and lenders.

If the company is *private*, the sellers might also qualify for reporting a portion of their gain until receipt of principal payments on their seller loans. For example, if the sellers take fifty percent of the total price in cash and fifty percent in loans, one half of the tax otherwise payable is deferred pending receipt of loan principal.

Sources of third-party capital include sales and leasebacks of acquired fixed assets, local community development loans, loans from Small Business lenders, loans from insurance companies, and factoring of accounts receivable.

In cases where significant growth opportunity exists, the use of an Initial Public Offering (IPO) merits detailed study. While large well-known companies often manage their own IPO, smaller companies generally use outside Investment Bankers (IBs) having large distribution networks.

The IBs due diligence is quite thorough. Companies wishing to complete an IPO often benefit from having their professionals perform pre-IPO due diligence to avoid surprise findings by the selected IB.

As mentioned in the Joint Venture section of Chapter 2, creating an arrangement with a third-party having assets, capital or business relationships with target suppliers or customers creates an attractive and hopefully efficient source of capital. Part of the attractiveness is that the arrangement is government by contract as opposed to securities law. Tax efficiency exists due to partnership (pass through) taxation.

Unless the company or its third-party professionals have quality contacts with third parties, the use of professionals focusing most of their time and efforts to capital raising often provides the most harmonious outcome.

CHAPTER 6

Sales Process

The chart shown on the following page is provided by Fogel Capital Partners, LLC and used with their permission. I am a member of this company and have worked with Ian Subel, one of its founding members, for many years.

I first met Ian when he sought a position with the firm's Los Angeles office. Ian was the youngest person ever admitted to the partnership of one of South Africa's largest Chartered Accountancy firms.

I never made a better hire the entire time I was leading the firm's Mergers & Acquisitions group. He is intelligent, hardworking and a real team player. I miss working with him on a daily basis.

Reasons for selling

The most common reason for family owned and operated businesses is that owners believe they will be better off selling and living off the net sales proceeds. This occurs for a variety of factors including:

- Lack of a successor operator

- Declining health or owner demise
- Owner/operator fatigue
- Lifestyle issues
- Family feud
- Taking advantage of a perceived premium valuation in market conditions

Publicly-owned companies sell for a variety of reasons including modifying strategic direction and focus. General Electric Company (GE)is, perhaps, the best domestic example. Offshore Companies include Anglo-American of London, UK, and Johannesburg South Africa (Anglo-American). Many years ago, Anglo-American owned Mondi Paper company in South Africa. As part of refining its strategic focus, it sold off its timber plantations and largely exited the pulp and paper business.

Before deciding to sell, owners of family owned businesses should carefully review what the company pays for that they must fund once a deal closes. Common items include medical, dental, and vision care for family members, company paid travel and entertainment, season tickets to sporting events, golf club memberships, and company paid donations to museums, zoos, opera, symphonies, theater groups, and orchestras. Once a sale closes these are paid by the sellers using their after income tax dollars.

In one transaction our sellers received a fantastic offer for their company. However, the deal made no sense to them as the after-tax proceeds would not support the sellers' lifestyles: they would have retired and run out of money within a short period after the sale.

For both private and public businesses, the sell decision should begin with strategic planning.

It is critical to understand you do not decide on Sunday to sell your company and go to market on Monday. If you decide to sell on Sunday you spend time critically reviewing your company and identifying necessary improvements required to obtain the best price.

In one deal named "reef" the company was implementing an SAP system costing in excess of $10m. We immediately had them cease the implementation as they would not get credit for costs involved and the benefits that the buyer received in later years.

Strategic Planning and Sales Strategy

Strategy development

Selling a business significantly impacts its stakeholders. For purposes of this discussion, stakeholders include owners, lenders, employees, customers, vendors and the community in which the business operates.

In many instances, sellers fail to estimate the impact on stakeholders and how such failure might impact transaction difficulty and the price obtainable. Deciding whether, when, and how stakeholders are informed is a key part of the strategic planning process.

If, after reviewing industry prospects, current state of the economy and, for private companies, any family estate and financial planning goals, the sell decision emerges as most advantageous, the sellers begin the marketing process.

Preparing the business for sale

Range of Values

The major steps of this process include determining a range of values for the business, looking at opportunities to enhance operating results including income and cash flow, and developing a strategy for investing after tax proceeds of the sale.

Outside Advisors

Determining value range is a crucial first step especially for the outside adviser. For example, if the sellers believe their company is worth $20m and the offers come in at $30m, the adviser has done a great job. However, if they believe their company is worth $40m the deal will probably go south as the seller thinks the offer is 25% below market value.

Determining reasonable sales price expectations is the best rationale for retaining outside expertise. Many sellers believe they can do it themselves. However, a good advisor often achieves a much better after-tax result by getting the transaction through due diligence, using the best structuring alternatives and, where possible, avoiding post transaction buyer audits.

In many cases, sellers and or their advisors combine operations analysis and range of values for purposes of determining an asking price.

They do this in the event they find a significant operations improvement that increases operating income and cash flow. While buyers might not wish to pay for something that may or may not happen, they might be amenable to a contingent payment payable once the anticipated improvement occurs.

Upon completion of balance sheet, income, and cash flow projections, one can develop a range of values for the business.

If it is a real estate business, the comparable companies might include publicly traded companies, including Real Estate Investment Trusts (REITs). Since privately-owned companies incur a discount for lack of liquidity relative to publicly-traded companies, this is only appropriate if the company is publicly traded. If it is not, one must look to book values and discounted cash flow analysis to determine range of values. One determines the rate of discount applicable to cash flows by reference to current market capitalization rates applied to the various categories of developed real estate.

If the business is engaged in a non-real estate operating business, a range of values is determinable by reference to publicly-traded business using similar business codes. (North American Industry Classification System (NAICS) code). If the company is not publicly traded, a liquidity discount applies.

For example, if the company operates a business generating $10 million in cash in an industry where public companies trade at seven times cash flow, the initial value is $70 million. Since the company lacks liquidity, a discount applies. Depending on the industry involved, this discount might be in the range of 20 to 30 percent. If the appropriate discount is 30 percent, the indicated value range approximates $49,000,000 (70 percent of $70 million).

Determining a value range is an art form. The company is generally worth more to some buyers than others. This is why identifying potential buyers is often the most important part of preparing a company for sale.

Based on my experience, I believe that, unless the owners have extensive contacts in the industry, they should use an outside advisor having such contacts. This advisor knows or can find out who might be the highest bidder and how to best present the opportunity.

In the current market most businesses are trading at multiples of normalized earnings (averaged over a period of years) before interest taxes depreciation and amortization (EBITDA); in some instances (especially software based businesses buyers often pay a multiple of average revenues

Operations Analysis and Improvement

This is an area where third-party professionals should add value since they are not part of the company's history and will not be at fault for overlooking profit or cost saving opportunities. They look for items such as deferred maintenance and owner specific expenses avoidable by a buyer, creating efficiencies in production, sales, marketing and distribution, and overhead expenses. The end product of this analysis is a restated set of projections and range of values based on decisions within the buyer's control. While a buyer might not agree with the projections, having them available provides a basis for negotiating contingent post sale payments. You cannot sell a business today without providing intelligent projections that you are able to substantiate (or you will end up with an earnout).

Personal Portfolio Planning

This task is best performed by a qualified investment advisor. While I have advised clients on investment strategy, I have no experience recommending specific investments and am not in this business.

Marketing Documents

Marketing documents include an Executive Summary/teaser (often on a no names basis), Non-Disclosure Agreement and Confidential Private Placement Memorandum.

Thoughts on language usage

Readers know these are marketing documents that have a seller favorable bias. Nothing is taken as factual until verification by due diligence.

Having read and helped prepare many of these kinds of documents, I believe they should: 1, avoid usage of exaggerated statements, and 2, use substantive language.

Hyperbole is a turnoff. In many cases readers will know enough about the industry or company to recognize factual exaggeration. They will either pass on the opportunity because of the anticipated due diligence required or move forward with great care, mistrust, and doubt.

Substantive words include nouns, pronouns, and verbs. They are real. Adjectives and adverbs modify substantives; in some cases, their usage causes readers to doubt the reality of the substantive. We all have a mental image of a mountain. When a writer uses the adjective beautiful with the word mountain, careful readers might question why the writer felt the need for modifying the noun. I agree and accept that most documents require modifiers. My point is that when used, you should take care to choose the most accurate modifier.

Executive Summary

This is a brief description of the company that includes its history, industry trends and dynamics. Most private companies do not disclose financial information other than year over year revenue and net income percentage changes. When appropriate, the executive summary sets forth growth opportunities available to new owners and the means for capturing them.

The target audience for the summary includes potential buyers who expressed interest in the past as well as those expected to have an interest.

The letter contains language to the effect that more detailed information is available to parties executing a non-disclosure agreement (NDA) and the method for securing the draft NDA.

Non-Disclosure Agreement

House or third-party counsel produce this document which is tailored for the specific transaction needs. The internet is an excellent source of sample forms useable for background reading together with key provisions used in most transactions.

Seller and their advisors should realize that competitors often request documents anonymously or through third parties to gain competitive information. All parties requesting information should be called asking why they want the information and whether they will be acting as principals.

Confidential Private Placement Memorandum

This document provides everything a prospective buyer should know about the company and its business.

Key components include:

- Company history including founders and operating locations
- Industry history, trends, competitors and the company's market share
- Key management information including biographies and tenure
- Identification of third-party outside experts including legal, accounting, finance, employee benefits, and other important relationships, including regulators, and industry consulting experts
- Existence of supplier and vendor agreement with average term
- Primary lender contact information
- Financial projections of Net Income, Balance Sheet, and Cash Flow for at least five years together with underlying assumptions
- Detailed product information including patent protections, brand protection programs, quality control techniques, key suppliers and significant customers
- Market development opportunities together with estimated capture cost
- Status of relationships with local government and trade associations
- Risk environment for the company and its industry together with mitigation techniques
- Tax audit history
- Lawsuit history
- Regulatory report summary
- For companies having offshore operations the memorandum

includes history, profitability, and relationship with the host country
- Anything potentially important to a buyer not noted above

There is an "art" to providing enough information to excite the buyer vs. not providing too much confidential Information on the assumption that this book will be reviewed by your biggest competitors.

In past years books were always hard copies numbered etc. to control dissemination. Today books are provided electronically using technology allowing for watermarking etc., to control dissemination.

Buyer Due Diligence

It is common practice today for sellers to set up a data room in the cloud using companies specializing in such services.

In smaller deals, a third-party location often houses the data room to minimize or eliminate employee (stakeholder) concerns. When using a physical data room sellers must

control things like what is presented to certain buyers, their ability to print copies, and watermarking prints etc. to maintain confidentiality.

When performing due diligence on site, I always asked how people wanted me to dress since someone new showing up in a suit sets off a mental alarm. The most unusual request asked me to dress as a Boeing Parts Buyer. Being clueless about what that meant, they told me khaki slacks, print long sleeve shirt, no tie or sport coat, sport shoes, and a pocket protector.

The NDA provides guidance with respect to whether prospective buyers may copy information in the data room.

The Confidential Private Placement Memorandum (PPM) forms a road map for buyer due diligence. Buyers expect to find whatever they need to understand and evaluate the company and its industry in the data room.

The data room or confidential cloud based facility used for due diligence should contain financial statements for all years contained in the PPM, all material contracts, all federal, state, local, and foreign tax returns for years contained in the PPM plus audit reports, any and all regulatory reports.

If the PPM claimed ability to enhance operating results, the data source has supporting documentation describing capital and resource requirements.

Management presentations are a critical part of diligence and are useable for disclosing information too confidential for disclosure in the book or dataroom]

Transaction Execution

Evaluate Alternative Offers

The best alternative is not always the one with the highest price. Tax structuring makes a lower price deal more attractive when after-tax cash flow exceeds that obtainable with the higher price deal.

This often occurs when assets are sold, giving the buyer higher tax basis in acquired assets, or when term debt allows for installment sale reporting for tax purposes.

A qualified tax professional should always participate in the review of alternative offers. Even where only one offer exists, this professional would suggest ways of structuring the deal to maximize after-tax cash flow.

For example, I worked on a transaction based in Northern California. We had two great offers. One was $29m and the buyer would maintain the company as-Is and the other was $35m but the strategic buyer planned on moving all operations to the Midwest; all employees would be terminated. Our Seller decided to go with the lower offer since he did not want his long-time employees to lose their jobs.

Negotiate Letter of Intent

The selected buyer sends a letter of Intent to purchase (LOI) for seller's review. This letter sets forth the purchase price, the means of payment (cash, debt, stock), time frame for accomplishing tasks, and closing date. Key LOI items include requested representations and warranties and, in many deals, a post-closing purchase price adjustment.

Sellers should resist post-closing purchase price adjustments unless they have confidence that their balance sheet, cash flows, and income statements will hold up under intense scrutiny.

Many years ago, a client called telling me he met with the Chairman of a company that wished to buy his business. I asked whether I might help by reviewing the proposed purchase contract. My client said he had known the Chairman for a long time and felt my review unnecessary. As part of this conversation, he stated that the Chairman requested that he "clean up" the balance sheet prior to closing. I unsuccessfully repeated my proposal that I review the contract.

After closing, my client called telling me that the contract he signed included a post-closing purchase price adjustment. He asked that I attend a meeting to review the adjustments with the acquirer's Chief Financial Officer CFO). It was not a great meeting. The CFO denied that the Chairman asked for a balance sheet cleanup. In my argument, I stated that no reasonable person would write down assets before closing a deal with a purchase price adjustment. The meeting was heated and became emotional. After a lengthy debate, I was able to reduce the purchase price adjustment by a bit more than fifty percent.

M&A professionals must understand that in many deals, the Chairman's role is that of the good cop; the CFO is most always the bad cop.

Negotiate Final Contract

The Final Contract (Contract) is another form of legal art. While everything in the contract has legal significance, much attention is given to buyer and seller representations and warranties. These often survive closing and provide for damage payments when breached.

In complicated transactions, the Contract provides methods of payment for breaches including usage of one or multiple baskets for determining the amount and timing of payments.

Closing

Closing takes place after both parties sign off on the contract. Closings usually take place at a mutually agreeable lawyer's office. Most transactions use wire transfers at closing. The key item being that everyone knows the local deadline for wires, generally 3:00 pm local time.

Alternative to a Sale

There is one sale alternative most applicable to family-owned businesses. This alternative might apply in situations where no family member wishes to continue operating the business.

If the company manufactures or produces a product, the plant and equipment used in manufacturing could be sold to a third party. The selling company retains a royalty interest in post-sale revenue. The company either distributes the sales proceeds to owners or reinvests them on the owners' behalf.

Royalties received constitute passive investment income which, if the company is a regular corporation (C Corporation), might subject the income to the twenty percent additional tax imposed on undistributed personal holding income. Sellers that can avoid this tax are entities that pass through their income, gains and losses to owners. This category includes partnerships, limited liability companies, and corporations subject to tax under Subchapter S (S Corporations).

Achieving this result often requires pre or post sale company restructuring.

An additional sale avoidance option includes hiring experienced management to operate the business on its owner's behalf.

In Conclusion

I hope you found the "how to" part of my book interesting and helpful.

As you read it, you realize we all cook with the same ingredients. The *art* involves selecting the best ingredients for each transaction.

The second part of **Mergers & Acquisitions Playbook** contains case studies which include comments on techniques suggested in the "how to" part of this book.

I wish you good luck as you move forward as part of this interesting and exciting practice.

CHAPTER 7

Working with Japanese Clients

Welcome to Los Angeles

I transferred to the Los Angeles office of one of the largest financial services firms in 1995 when I became the founding partner of its M&A Strategy Consulting Group.

Several people-oriented reasons convinced me that I should make the transfer from Dallas. During my visits there, I met Frank T the Managing Partner of the firm's Western Region. He is the best manager of people I ever had the opportunity to work with.

When people became aware of my transfer Bertha A, who had been assistant to the Tax Partner in Charge, said I would need an assistant and should choose her. I was pleased that she wished to be my assistant but asked "why her". She said I should because she knew all of the people in the office worth knowing. That was the beginning of a great friendship that lasted until the day she passed.

The third people-oriented reason was Tom I, a Japanese American who ran the firm's Asia practice. Without his guidance and contacts, I would not have enjoyed my successful experience of working with Japanese clients.

Cultural Awareness 101

Before moving to Los Angeles, I never focused on cultural awareness. I quickly learned that having such awareness is fundamental to participating in global transactions. In addition to his business acumen, Tom made sure I was aware of the finer points of Japanese business culture.

He told me that when you visited a Japanese office, you are seated facing the door. I suppose this began during the Samurai era; enabling visitors to see who might be (welcome or not) joining them.

He said that when I was in a meeting with Japanese businessmen, the person in the middle of their side of the table doing most of the talking was not the most important. The most important was the older guy at either end doing the listening.

Tom's experience was American business people were, by Japanese standards, loud and rude. He suggested that I would do best by talking softly and never using the word "no." I did learn that saying something on the order of, "that might be difficult," constitutes "no" in Japanese.

According to Tom, Japanese companies, at least back then, had a concept of honor relative to trading with American companies. This meant that, if they made a publicly-announced deal, they would not accept other offers unless the other party backed out. It also meant that if they were selling a company, they would not accept an offer deemed too low to be honorable. In those cases, they would sell to management with no down payment and provide sufficient cash flow to run the business for two years so that it would not go bankrupt during their ownership.

In Tokyo addresses use numbers given by the order in which each building was erected in the prefecture. Number 1 is almost never next to number 2. Tom's advice was having the client text or email the address in Japanese for use by the taxi driver.

The key "take away" from this is whenever you begin working on a cross border transaction you must find someone to mentor you on the culture of that country. Business ethics often vary by country. What is considered as "shady" in one country might be considered as "normal" in other countries. A primer by someone versed in the country's culture can help avoid expensive mistakes.

Golf Course Experience

A good example of cultural differences includes a transaction where a bank held the debt on a Bankrupt Golf(BG)property.

A group executed a contract to buy the golf course property for an amount vastly exceeding the face amount of the debt. This was great news for the bank since they would be paid in full and collect any accrued and unpaid interest.

A large publicly owned company called the bank's advisor to inform him that they wished to a "topping" bid using the bank's advisor to submit the bid on its letterhead.

Upon arrival they gave a check payable to the advisor's firm for $100,000. The payment was for the advisor to submit an introduction on the firm's letterhead together with their bid. The advisor was reluctant to do this since the bank might interpret this as attempt to have them dishonor the publicly announced transaction. When the advisor stated that he did not wish to send the letter, the public company's representatives threatened to inform the advisors chairman of his refusal to assist a large client of the advisors firm. After thinking about how he would manage any fallout from sending the bid letter the advisor emailed the bid with hard copy to follow.

Later that night the advisor received a call telling him to be on the next plane to the client's location.

The bank was very unhappy since they did not wish to be perceived as doing something dishonorable.

The advisor told the bank that he was not asking them to do anything dishonorable but was sending the bid because it was from a well-qualified buyer and could be used if and when the group's contract failed to close.

After returning, the advisor estimated the cost of being "chewed out" for creating the potential for dishonor at a little over $72,000. This incident showed how much honor and being honorable meant to Japanese businesses. This knowledge served the advisor well in a beef company transaction where the seller was Japanese.

CHAPTER 8

Beef Company Transaction

A Buy Side Transaction with Japanese Seller

Background Information

A company in the Pacific Northwest. had a subsidiary they wished to sell. After researching the relevant industry, the my team prepared a pitch showing our industry knowledge as well as steps we would take to find a buyer and help with deal structuring, negotiation, and closing.

Three days after our presentation, we received a phone call from the COO telling that our proposal was the best, but he could not us since we had yet to receive our broker dealer license. He ended the conversation by stating that he would need us in the future.

About a year later and after I retired, the COO called telling me had become the Board Chair and wanted my help with due diligence, transaction structuring and negotiation.

The Company, (AB) is located in the Northwestern US. According to information provided by senior management, AB was formed in 1978 for the purpose of managing five feedlots owned by the founder and another person in the business. The reason for its formation was managing accounting and finance and cattle and grain procurement.

In the early days, AB was in a JV with other producers and a packing plant. This venture made sense for all parties since, in some fiscal quarters the producers made money, but the packers incurred losses and in others the opposite occurred. The joint venture minimized the volatility for the participants. It lasted for about ten years and fell apart due to competing agendas. AB always believed a packing component was necessary for its long-term industry viability.

AB acquired the Wagyu genetics several years earlier than my involvement. Their premium product involved crossing Wagyu Bulls with Black Angus cows, creating fantastic brisket, steak varieties and hamburger.

The Opportunity

An individual AB worked with in the past let them know that a beef packing plant in the State of Washington, and which was a subsidiary of a Japanese Company was on the market. AB hired me adv to assist with due diligence, structuring, preparing an offer letter and contract, and price negotiations.

AB's on-site due diligence team included Robert R (Chairman and CEO), Bill R (CFO), Rick S (VP Business Development), Dwight P (third-party industry consultant) and me. They and I met in Seattle then drove to the plant to interview key management and review documentation.

The company was on the market due to its long history of operating losses due, in large part, to its cattle raising business. A brief meeting with the COO revealed its principle cause. He came to work every day in a blue pin stripe suit, white shirt, tie, and black shoes and had not been in the packing plant for more than four years. I was unable to pin down what he viewed as his job description, but, in his mind, it clearly did not include managing the business for its owners.

The packing plant is on an Indian Reservation and subject to some of its rules. A key for retaining water required offering all job openings to members of the tribe before considering outside parties. At the time of our due diligence, no member of the tribe ever accepted a job.

Since the plant is subject to regulation by the Environmental Protection Agency (EPA), Food and Drug Administration (FDA), and the United States Department of Agriculture (USDA), obtaining available background information was a key due diligence component. In addition to financial due diligence, the team devoted significant time and effort to purchase and supply contracts, employee benefit plans, employee performance evaluations, annual employee turnover and the relationship of the company with the various unions having workers at the plant.

Early in the process, I met with the seller's broker; after advising my client about my proposal, the broker and I agreed on a formula for determining the sales price. Since the company continually lost money, the formula was the book value at the month end before we began due diligence plus or minus accumulated income or losses as of the month end prior to closing.

A short time after signing off on the formula, he called accusing me of cheating his client (his wording was a bit stronger) by including depreciation in accumulated profits or losses and asked me to revise it. My response was that there was no way I was going back to my client to make a change because he failed to understand the document he signed. After consulting with my client, I revisited the issue with the broker; agreement was made to drop the formula and negotiate a price upon completion of due diligence.

There was a lot of "hair" on this deal. The most problematic were potential issues with the Yakima Tribe, regulatory (no recent EPA or FDA reports), pending union contract negotiations, finding experienced senior operating management, establishing distribution and supply systems, upgrading the plants information technology systems, and integrating the plant into AB's operations. Despite the hair, AB decided to move forward due to the strategic need to acquire a packing plant and the prospect of an attractive purchase price.

All parties met in Seattle in late March 2003 for purposes of negotiating the final price.

At 4:30 my brother called, telling me That our father died earlier that day.

I met briefly with the seller's broker and my client, telling them the reason for my early departure. About three days after my father's funeral, the seller's broker called asking whether AB remained interested. I said they were; we agreed to meet in Seattle about a week later to conclude negotiations.

AB brought legal counsel to the meeting. After several hours, I believed the price on the table was as low as we wished to go since a lower price would be deemed dishonorable by the Japanese seller. AB's lawyer argued that we could go lower as the sellers had no alternative. I replied that they did. Their alternative was to sell the business to management, providing one hundred percent low interest debt financing and sufficient cash flow to carry the business for two years. My client agreed. AB purchased the assets at a low enough price that it was recovered by operating cash flow within the following twelve months. Tom I's advice served me well.

Over the years, AB made significant improvements and upgrades to the plant. It can process nearly twice as much product than was the case when acquired.

About four years after acquiring the plant, AB acquired a ranch near Loomis, WA., and changed its name to Double R Ranch in honor of R R Sr., founder of the family business.

According to R R, the ranch acquisition brought AB back to its "roots". It provided the company with a geographic spot to further focus/develop its genetic base and strengthen its vertically integrated market position.

AB sells it's the most of its premium brand, to the finest grocery stores and restaurants in the Pacific Northwest. What is not sold there is sold to fine restaurants around the United States.

The Double R Ranch and St. Helens premium Black Angus, brands enjoy a great following in restaurants and grocery stores in the same region.

I highlighted this transaction as an outstanding example of a company analyzing its strengths and weaknesses; then developing a clear strategy for achieving long term market stability and financial viability. AB achieved this without significant use of third-party consultants.

CHAPTER 9

Perils of Falling in Love with an Opportunity

In Chapter 2 I mentioned the importance of not falling in love with a deal.

Years ago, a financial buyer requested assistance with reviewing a regional movie theater chair offered for sale by a Hollywood Producer.

I circulated copies of the offering documents among my group. The tax professionals looked for tax opportunities and pitfalls as well as at potential tax structuring alternatives. I focused on operating due diligence.

After my third read through, I went back to the section dealing with trends in movie screen costs and revenue per screen. Over the previous 5 years the cost per screen increased by an increasing rate while revenue per screen decreased by an increasing rate. While I was not an industry expert this factor, together with the fact that it was on offer from an industry professional, seemed troublesome.

Rather than merely discussing this with our client's person in charge, I prepared a graph showing the trend lines. As an aside, whenever possible and appropriate, I use visual presentations since it is nearly always true that pictures speak more clearly than text or spoken words.

When I asked what had peaked his firm's interest in the deal. He replied that teasers were sent to all of the buyout groups and various strategic buyers and most decided to perform due diligence as it seemed an attractive opportunity. The advisor asked how his firm felt about the fact that the seller was a Hollywood insider. He replied that the view of most auction participants, including his firm, was that this was the beginning of a trend to separate the film production part of the industry from its bricks and mortar component.

After that part of the discussion, I requested the client's views on the pitch book and whether he noted any red flags. He mentioned some concern about the fact that most of the revenue going to theater owners came from food and beverage sales, with very little earned from ticket sales.

The I showed him my graph. The client went to the pitch book pages shown as his graph's source and said he failed to understand the text's significance upon first reading. He said we should keep working on the deal pending discussions with his New York office. About one hour after lunch, he told me they were not proceeding and we should send a bill for work done up to that point.

It was once widely believed that if Berkshire Hathaway showed interest in a public company its value increased by around 20 percent. Similarly, if the largest buyout firms expressed interest in a deal, its market value increased, creating potential for a frenzied auction. Everyone loved the deal because the "smart" money was all in.

One of the largest buyout firms made the winning bid. They had to place the movie chain into bankruptcy within three years from date of purchase.

The point of this chapter is that while knowing what other parties think or believe is usually worthwhile, this knowledge is best used for setting a frame of reference and not as a guiding light.

You must think for yourself and stay focused on industry metrics. The fact that cost per screen was increasing while revenue per screen decreased was far more important than the identity of the other bidders.

CHAPTER 10

Community Newspapers

Two newspaper industry professionals decided the time was right to buy community newspapers, including those offering weekly and daily subscriptions.

One of the principals worked for the Washington Post during the Pentagon Papers era. After leaving The Post he became editor of the Denver Post, where he met the other principal who was a sports reporter for the paper.

After working together for several years, they decided they could make more money owning papers than by working for other owners. While searching for acquisition candidates they found an attractive candidate located in the southern part of Colorado.

They were sufficiently far along with the negotiations that they knew the purchase price which was acceptable to them. Since they were not cash buyers they

sought financial advice and transaction assistance from my firm.

I told them I would need to perform due diligence on them before accepting them as clients. This due diligence included searching all kinds of public records, interviewing previous employers, speaking with their legal counsel and income tax preparers.

I mention this due diligence because some advisors fail to perform due diligence on prospective clients. A failure to do this can damage the firm's reputation and often has legal and financial consequences.

The timing was two years before the real estate bubble burst in Dallas; loans were easily obtained and relatively low cost. The ultimate price for the paper approximated $4.0 million; I found a bank loan for $3.9 million. They were in business for an out of pocket investment approximating $50,000 each.

Less than a year later, they found a chain of community newspapers forming a ring around Houston, TX. I went back to the same bank that made the loan on the Colorado property. I told them the transaction was in the $6 million range and asked if they had interest.

They asked how much my clients were putting down. My response was if their bank wished to be part of the deal they would provide 100% financing. They agreed, saying that if there was a next deal, they would require equity. The clients, surprised that they did not have to put more of their cash in the deal, were happy to agree.

In the 1980s the Dallas real estate bubble burst. Upon learning that their lender was nearing default, I visited with a principal with a buyout firm. They bought the debt. Their fee consisted of receiving purchase rights.

Subsequent to the 1980s additional community newspapers became part of the portfolio.

When the papers sold, the buyout fund received full payment on the debt plus nearly $1 million on the rights. The clients were multi-millionaires.

Their return on equity was huge.

This deal is another example of strategy development without use of paid advisors. The clients were industry professionals who, based on more than 60 years of in depth industry experience, performed the operations due diligence.

The advisor's value adds included: 1) obtaining favorable loans, 2) structuring the entity owning the assets in a way that the its assets, as opposed to equity in the owning entity, could be sold. Since an asset sale allowed the new owners to claim higher depreciation deductions than would have been possible in an equity sale, they paid a significantly higher purchase price.

This chapter shows that additional value is achievable if you use your knowledge, skill, and intellectual curiosity to find ways to improve transaction economics. Moreover, structuring is incomplete until you have: included downside protection and upside potential into the structure.

CHAPTER 11

Working with Entrepreneurs

In addition to the community newspaper transactions, I worked on several transactions with entrepreneurs. Working with people who founded their company is significantly different from working with buyout funds or strategic buyers. Entrepreneurs are so excited about the prospects for their new business or, when selling, expecting to reap huge financial rewards.

The first involved finding investors for a startup company.

The second was the sale of a company by its founder.

As I summarize each transaction I explain why they are included.

Mr. Micro

Martin L. (Marty) emigrated from South Africa in 1977. Before emigrating, he researched Commercial Metals Company (CMC) and believed they would hire him to trade various South African products; creating a new product line for CMC.

My recollection is that Marty cold called CMC asking for a meeting with Jacob Feldman its founder and largest shareholder.

They must have been a great meeting as he was hired immediately and began working on trades of building materials sourced in South Africa.

Marty asked Mr. Feldman for referrals to a lawyer and accountant. Happily, they referred him to me and I became his advisor.

Given Marty's intellectual curiosity and high energy level I was not surprised when he brought me a TRS 80: a new minicomputer with a tape drive. He told me he had been visiting Tandy Corporation in Ft. Worth, Texas. They gave him several TRS 80s to use as demos; he gave one to me to try out.

A short time later, Apple entered the business with its first table top mac and Texas Instruments (TI) opened its first retail computer store at the Northpark Mall in Dallas, Texas.

Marty asked me to visit TI's retail store in a major Dallas shopping mall. Upon entering the store, I noted that there was one salesperson and no inventory on display. This meant that there were no computers for buyers to test at the store. The salesperson had a list of components available for purchase but lacked the training necessary to give purchase advice. The only people able to shop at this store needed to know what they needed and how to connect purchased components.

Marty had a better idea.

His plan was a retail store where there were many computers set up and immediately useable. His salespeople would take children to working computers so parents could see them begin performing tasks on computers in the store. He would only sell Apple computers.

Marty told me he would give me a piece of the company I found financing.

Fortunately, I had friends at a large corporation located in Dallas. I visited the senior executives and told them about Marty's plan for a company retailing Apple Computers (Mr. Micro). They agreed to meet Marty to discuss his business plan.

The meeting exceeded Marty and my expectations. After completing his pitch, Marty briefly left the room. They asked me if I thought the company would succeed. I replied that there were no guarantees, but if hard work, intelligence, and integrity were enough for that kind of business, it would succeed.

They made the investment which was sufficient to obtain a lease for Mr. Micro's first retail location, find and train qualified staff, and purchase inventory.

On Mr. Micro's opening weekend it sold its entire inventory. The company was profitable from day one. A second retail location opened with equal success. Prior to its being sold, Mr. Micro was the largest independent Apple retailer in the Southwestern United States.

A larger company purchased Mr. Micro. Marty, his investors, and I did very well as the after-tax proceeds exceeded everyone's expectations. The downside for Marty was a non-compete agreement.

During the time his non-compete agreement was in effect, Marty's wife, Rozlyn, worked for a business recruiting firm specializing in contract and permanent placements. At the non-competes termination, they formed ExPerTalent which specialized in recruiting and permanent placements of Information Technology professionals. You cannot keep entrepreneurs down.

During this process Marty became a great friend. I have great respect for his intelligence, professionalism, and integrity.

Unlike many entrepreneurs, he delegated well while providing the amount of guidance required. He wanted his business to grow and only hired people having the potential to be as good as or better than him since that approach would help his company grow faster.

I included this deal as it shows what an intelligent well-rounded entrepreneur can achieve with financial help. Keys to entrepreneurial success include delegation skills, guidance, integrity, high energy level, and the willingness to hire people with like or superior skills without fear of being overshadowed.

Glove Company
Western United States

One of my associates sold a project to sell a medical glove company (GC) in the Western United States. The seller was the GC's founder and an entrepreneur.

We helped the seller prepare an Executive Summary, Pitch Book, and other marketing materials and assisted house counsel with important documents including the non-disclosure agreement form. We also briefed our client with talking points for the management presentations that are part of due diligence.

We found three interested parties within sixty days. From these, the GC received three requests for copies of the Pitch Book. Two of the three signed documents allowing them to begin due diligence.

We helped GC set up a data room at our office. After each potential buyer completed due diligence, GC received two bids and selected one. Within two weeks we had a signed purchase and sale agreement.

The high bidder, a financial buyer, needed to borrow about one half of the purchase price. Their lender performed its due diligence at the same time as the buyer and provided a support letter indicating its ability and willingness to provide the required funds.

The scheduled closing was to occur in New York on the third Friday after both parties and the lender signed binding agreements. I asked my associate to attend the closing.

About 3 pm, my associate came to my office telling me the deal did not close. When I asked why, he told me the GC owner got into a fight with the lender's representative. I asked why he failed to calm things down. He told me he could not because he did not attend the closing. When I asked why, he told me the owner did not wish to pay for our time and travel, refusing to let him attend.

I almost lost it, but told him he should have let me know of our client's request so that I could intervene. It is fundamental in this business that advisors attend closings since issues often arise that advisors are most competent to resolve.

About four days after the scheduled closing, I called our client asking if he was serious about selling or had seller's remorse. He said he was but the lender was a jerk. I said it takes two jerks to start a fight. I told him I would work the deal personally.

I was able to get the buyer and lender back on track. The dates were the only changes to the original contract. We arranged to close the following Friday in New York.

Prior to closing, I called the New York law firm, requesting that my client be on a separate floor in the building from the lender's representative (Banker). This worked quite well as the Banker and my client did not meet until the closing party.

The evening before closing, I walked the streets of Manhattan with my client trying to get him think about whether he really wanted to sell his company. He said he would sign the papers in the morning.

He seemed anxiously cheerful in the morning. The banker signed off on the documents but my client told me he had to read every word even though the only changes were to dates. Alarmed that he might try to delay closing I arranged for the wires to come from Wells Fargo in San Francisco.

About 3:15 New York time, he handed me the documents and said that the wire transfers would have to wait until Monday. I told him we would close today since I was using Wells Fargo in San Francisco. I also told him I had checks for the $100k bonuses for his house counsel and controller. When he asked why I did this, I told him I thought he might forget to make the payments. I delivered the checks to his bonus recipients.

The closing occurred at the 21 Club in New York. My client and the banker appeared to be BFFs.

I included this as another example of working with entrepreneurs.

In this transaction the client lacked communication skills and had, in my opinion, trust issues. Since he was unsure of his end game he was a reluctant seller. I also learned that, as in most endeavors, you must be a part-time therapist.

CHAPTER 12

Working with Strategic Buyers

A strategic buyer is an acquirer in the same industry or business as its target. As opposed to financial buyers, strategic buyers look

for businesses to integrate with its main operations. Strategic buyers often pay an acquisition premium for hoped-for synergies. The value and probability that each strategic buyer assigns to synergies varies with the likelihood that the synergies occur.

Public companies that are strategic buyers include General Electric, Amazon, Microsoft, Apple, Banks, Utilities, and Social Media Companies.

The larger strategic buyers usually have full-time M&A professionals on staff. In most cases they only work with third parties that provide deal flow, specialized knowledge and skills, and the ability to make introductions. These parties are usually large investment banks or specialty consulting firms such as McKinsey& Co.

There are many small strategic buyers who primarily use third-party consultants. When AB CO. purchased Washington Beef, they acted as strategic buyers. Their outside advisers were my firm, RAB Financial Advisors, LLC., And Dwight P an individual having deep meat packing industry skills.

I participated in several public company strategic deals including public utilities, banks, and telecommunications. My value adds in these included tax structuring including reorganizations and limited operations due diligence.

A private company hired me for due diligence and tax structuring for five transactions involving its consolidation of family-owned grocery stores on the California coast.

My most interesting and, for the firm, my most profitable strategic buyer deal occurred a large East Coast bank (ECB) acquired a Texas bank out of bankruptcy.

I mentioned this transaction in my discussion dealing with the implausibility of merging two underperforming companies and hoping for a great result.

Prior taking down the bank down, the Federal Reserve (FED) offered and perhaps promised the deal to a highly qualified individual. He was very surprised and upset when the FED gave what he believed to have been his deal to ECB.

In fact, he was so upset he formed an Equity Committee (EC) in an attempt to gain value for his team and the Bank's shareholders. His lawyers hired my firm for the reorganization and tax work.

I suppose that ECB's due diligence people failed to notice that, unlike many large banks, a holding company owned the banks and non-banking subsidiaries. This failure created a large financial and monetary problem for ECB.

I checked out the Bank's prior year consolidated tax returns. After reading the applicable tax regulations, I found that the Holding

Company (HC) which benefited the participants included in the Equity Committee (EC) was responsible for filing the consolidated tax returns and making applicable tax elections so long as the Bank remained in bankruptcy. I also discovered that based on its tax loss for the year, it was entitled to about $60 million of the refund attributable to that year's operating loss.

I called the Bank's tax director telling him that we controlled the filing of the tax returns. His reply was the FED's tax person had control. I told him the FED's person was wrong and asked that he set up a conference call among the three of us. After reading the applicable regulations, they agreed with me.

I told the FED's tax person that, unless ECB agreed in writing to give the HC its portion of the refund, I would file an election to carry the loss forward in which case it would disappear as part of the bankruptcy process.

The final day for filing the return was September 15th. I requested an electronic copy of the return on September 10th; I received it on the 13th. There were more than 100 subsidiaries and there had been a short year during the year. This meant there were over 200 columns in the tax return.

I rounded up everyone not working on something to be filed on the 15th and had them load information in our Osborne Computers. My people worked all night, went home, showered and returned for another all-nighter. Around 11am on the 15th one of my people told me they would never finish because the Osborne Computers were overloaded causing our people to delete items cell by cell. I asked them to keep at it.

Around 1pm on the 15th the FED's tax person called; jokingly asking how long until we finished. I told him we were sending people home and would have the return to the Post Office before 5pm. Thirty minutes letter ECB's lawyer called asking us HC's counsel to bring the agreement for their signature. I would have sent something to the Post Office even if it was incomplete. The election to carry the loss forward made it sufficiently complete.

HC needed the Bankruptcy Court's permission to get the refund. Two groups were in opposition, the secured bondholders and the unsecured creditors.

Both groups were opposed since the refund to the HC would be out of their pockets. The bonds were paying over 10% and purchased for less than 20 cents on the dollar. They did not want the bankruptcy to end until they received everything recoverable. The unsecured creditors actually wanted the bankruptcy to end with them sharing recoverable proceeds with the secured bondholders. I believe they would have negotiated something between themselves.

At the tax refund confirmation hearing I prepared a chart showing the outcome. If the secured bondholders prevailed the HC received nothing. If the Bankruptcy Court chose the unsecured creditors proposal, the HC received about $35 million. The bar chart contained 3 columns: one with $0, one with $35 and one with $65.

While being examined under oath, the Unsecured Creditors' lawyer testified that my calculations were incorrect based on calculations made by their CPA experts. I asked why they believed I was wrong and was told that I was using the wrong regulation. I replied that their CPAs were not using the proper regulation and gave them the proper regulation. When their lawyer looked at their CPA expert, he looked at the regulation I cited and shrugged his shoulders, agreeing that he was incorrect. The lawyer was irritated at the shrug and dropped his argument.

My testimony was to the effect that the refund belonged to the HC and should go to shareholders and other members of the Equity

Committee. I also clearly stated that $60 million was more than $35 million and a whole lot more than Zero.

The presiding Judge said we would take a lunch break and he would rule after lunch.

After lunch, the Judge repeated my analysis and approved the request of the EC. As the result of the EC refund we received a $1 million bonus from the EC.

We learned a bit later that ECB's people illegally removed documents from the HC's locked safe deposit box. When our people reported this to the EC which took the matter to the Judge additional financial sums were distributed to the EC.

The following year we still controlled the tax return filing. I ask ECB's tax person (he was with the Bank before the reorganization) what number he wished to use for loan losses. He told me I would have to talk to house counsel. When I called her she told me, rather rudely, that she had no useful response.

At that time, all I could do was check the newspaper reporting at the time the Bank was taken down by the FED. According to contemporaneous articles the loans were worth about 15 cents on the dollar. Based on that information I wrote the loans down by $3.1 billion and filed the return. In its next financial quarter ECB lowered its previously announced earnings by $1.1 billion.

Shortly thereafter the senior person at ECB asked me to meet him at his office. When I arrived, he asked me to come over to the window. While I was there he said "see that man down there?" I asked which one; he said, "it doesn't matter."

He asked me to sit in front of his desk. When I sat, he said he understood the first $60 million since I was doing my job. But to reduce future cash flow by $1.1 billion was mean. He asked whether I was familiar with the indemnification provided by the FED. When I said I was not he told me that due to the indemnification he could go down to street level and shoot anyone and the FED would make it go away.

I replied that it was a great indemnification and I would ask HC legal counsel for an opinion. I explained that I called their tax director and would have used any number he wished. The tax director said I should call ECB's house counsel who refused to provide guidance and that, lacking any guidance from his personnel I used what had been publicly available. He picked his phone and fired his house counsel.

He said he would not apologize because he was too angry. I replied that is probably would not be a good idea for me to apply for any kind of loan from the Bank. He agreed with my statement.

I included this as an example of a transaction where the buyer, ECB, did not give adequate attention to tax aspects of bankruptcy reorganizations. Someone dropped the ball. This failure cost ECB something over $1.1 billion in cash.

Another reason for its inclusion is to point out that nothing should ever be assumed. HC's due diligence people assumed there were no tax issues. A short time after the merger, my firm received a $1 million bonus from the EC. When two of my tax partners asked how we could get a bonus in a bankruptcy My response was that, rather than merely filing tax returns, we should always tried to find ways to add value.

Conclusion

At the beginning of this book, I stated that M&A consulting is always about adding, preserving, and protecting value. This is fundamental to everything worthwhile in life.

It applies not only to financial matters, but includes our emotions, ideals, and our personal relationships. Anything worthwhile should be added to, preserved and protected.

When something does not work, keep ringing bells until you find the bell that works for you.

Acknowledgements

Five people made important contributions to my book.

Robert R and Bill R provided important background information for the beef packing plant acquisition.

My brother, Eric Boysen, made very constructive suggestions that made this book more easily readable than it might have been.

My wife, Patricia Boysen, upon reading the first two chapters told me she did not think anyone would understand me. That caused immediate revisions.

Ian Subel, a long-time friend and business partner observed that many things changed since we last worked together. Had he not told me, I would not have known that data rooms are most often cloud based.

www.ingramcontent.com/pod-product-compliance
Lightning Source LLC
Chambersburg PA
CBHW031535210526
45464CB00003B/1025